C000264935

Walking *with* Angels

Walking with Angels

Poems to *uplift* and *inspire*

Claire-Louise Price

Copyright © 2015 Claire-Louise Price

The moral right of the author has been asserted.

Apart from any fair dealing for the purposes of research or private study,
or criticism or review, as permitted under the Copyright, Designs and Patents
Act 1988, this publication may only be reproduced, stored or transmitted, in
any form or by any means, with the prior permission in writing of the
publishers, or in the case of reprographic reproduction in accordance with
the terms of licences issued by the Copyright Licensing Agency. Enquiries
concerning reproduction outside those terms should be sent to the publishers.

Matador
9 Priory Business Park,
Wistow Road, Kibworth Beauchamp,
Leicestershire. LE8 0RX
Tel: (+44) 116 279 2299
Fax: (+44) 116 279 2277
Email: books@troubador.co.uk
Web: www.troubador.co.uk/matador

ISBN 978 1784623 272

British Library Cataloguing in Publication Data.
A catalogue record for this book is available from the British Library.

Typeset in 11pt Aldine by Troubador Publishing Ltd, Leicester, UK

Matador is an imprint of Troubador Publishing Ltd

For Philip, forever.

Contents

Walking with Angels

Foreword

I didn't realise that my poems reflected a journey until they were gathered together and arranged in sequence for this book. Before that, they lived in various places around the house, most of them scribbled on scraps of paper or Post-it notes, or the proverbial back of an envelope, and either stuffed in a drawer or languishing in random notebooks in a box. It is time they saw the light of day.

Lightness, brightness and hope turned out to be common themes. I had doodled my first poem – 'Maybe' – shortly before a momentous life-changing event took place. My husband was diagnosed with a terminal brain tumour in 2009 and given months to live. Fortunately for us and our family of three sons, he defied the odds and continued to enjoy a remarkably high quality of life for four years before he died, peacefully, in 2013.

During these four years, we were living with the knowledge that the end of his life might come at any time. And yet, isn't that the same for us all? In a funny way, it was a privilege to be put 'on notice'. Life was brought into sharp focus and perspective. Life was for living right now, and in as an enriching way as possible. We talked, philosophised and enjoyed ourselves. We discovered cruises, explored Italy by train, bought a flat in Bath, tried new activities. I started my own freelance business to give us more flexibility while his supportive company relished having him back as a part time adviser.

In February 2012 a scan showed that the tumour had returned and yet by the summer it seemed to have been beaten again. During this period I started rehearsals as a volunteer performer in the London 2012 Olympics Opening Ceremony, something which I had got involved in purely by chance. I was cast as a dancing nurse in the NHS section. That was a delightful yet humbling experience. Many of my fellow performers were NHS doctors, nurses and workers. They saw human drama every working day. Keeping quiet about my personal situation helped me enjoy every rehearsal while my husband, determined to live long enough to see me take part, stayed stable and asymptomatic for a good few months after the Olympic Games ended.

Sometimes I needed to get away for a few days. The two poems 'The Olive Tree' and 'Walking with Angels' were written at two of Lynne Franks' BLOOM retreats in Deia, Majorca.

All the poems, based on my deep life experience, are offered to enrich, inspire and console. If there is just one which resonates with you, or someone you know, then I am content. And if you are inspired to follow your dream please don't wait. Do it now.

Claire-Louise Price
March 2015

Walking with Angels

Maybe

Maybe…
Who knows?
Like a leaf
Caught in the swirling wind
Round and round it goes
A thought in my head becomes
A decision.
Not 'now'
Not 'never'
Not 'sometime'
Just…
'Maybe'

Emergency

Blue light
Flashing bright
In the dark
Of the night
Siren blaring
Driving fast
How long will
This nightmare last?

Hold his hand tight
Pray he'll be all right
Keep calm like the crew
They know what to do
Not much time to spare
Luckily we make it there.

Blue light
Flashing bright
In the dark
Of the night
Pull right over
And give way
It could be you
Or yours one day.

Safe Haven

High upon the Dorset cliffs
We sit in sunlight and admire
An endless vista of sea and windswept sky
Blending into the horizon.
Not far from land,
Protected by a rocky promontory
We count thirty sailboats
Bobbing and darting across the water
Enjoying Sunday.
And in a while
Sated with the view
Shielded by the gorse from wind and walkers' gaze
We lie back on the springy turf,
Celebrating in our safe haven
Thirty years of married bliss
In one long, lingering kiss.

Seriously Frivolous

One morning I painted my nails bright pink
Shallow, superfluous, daft you might think
But after what happened that grey winter's day
Your frowns at frivolity will fade away:
With one last glance at my bright fingertips
He went off to work with a smile on his lips
The smile stayed with him and lifted his mood;
Though sorely provoked he declined to be rude
To the Big Boss wanting to axe someone's head
So – the troublemaker got fired instead.
That made a difference to working conditions
He started to shine, he lost inhibitions
His temper improved, his confidence grew
We were happy again in a way we once knew
Our family thrived, didn't go off the rails
And all 'cos one morning I painted my nails.

The Delight of Bath

Georgian City
Very pretty
Golden crescents, leafy squares
Take the waters
Take your daughters
Shopping there – but have a care
They won't find it very hard
To max out your credit card.

As for husbands, lovers, men
All will want to stay again
Rugby clubs and gastropubs
Cultural gems and shortened hems
Buzzing bars on Friday night
Revellers who rarely fight.

Bathonians are worldly wise
Creative, charming, civilised
Custodians of a Heritage Site
They make an effort, get it right
Tourists flock from far and near
This jewel is on our doorstep here
Eighty minutes from Paddington
A train will whisk you to the fun.

The Path of Life – *Dancers in White*

The Path of Life

It's not how we end up and where
It's what we did, and to whom, going there
It's not that we all end up dead
It's what we gave, how we smiled, what we said.
How should we measure success?
Not by money, nor status, nor dress
There's no reason, or logic, or rhyme
Our lives affect others all the time;
That chance word, friendly look or kind act
Can have a dramatic impact
We might have forgotten it fast
But for others the memory will last.
Acts of kindness do not count for nought
And that is a comforting thought
They are treasured by strangers and friends
And remembered long after life ends.

Gone

The house is quite sparkling
As neat as a pin
The rooms are all tidy
When we go in.

The furniture's gleaming
The lampshades are straight
The ham and cheese sandwich
Is still on the plate.

The back door looks polished
No scratches from claws
Our wellies stand straight
No mud on the floors.

The washing line billows
With sheets all along
The garden is pristine –
Our dog has gone.

The Pub Philosopher

What did that bloke Herrick say?
'Gather rosebuds while ye may'
This simple line of poetry
Eloquently speaks to me

The sword of Damocles hangs there
Suspended by a single hair
I see it now above the bar
It doesn't have to drop too far

And if it falls and strikes me dead
I don't want this thought in my head
'I wish I'd never worried so'
What a silly way to go

Oops sorry love, I broke your glass
I didn't mean to turn so fast
That poet's right, the truth he told
I'll drink to him and hit the road.

The Olympian

I met him at St Pancras
Straight off the train
How could I not?
'At times like this
He needs me'
Or so I thought.

Olympic hopes dashed
By stronger players
He'd helped to recruit
Only to be outshone
Now dropped from the team
And sent home.

He strode along the platform
Towards the barrier
Months of training
Had honed his physique
But the kit bag he shouldered
Was heavy with disappointment.

We went for a coffee
And a sandwich
In a café
On the Euston Road.
I remarked on the weather
Unsure what to say.

'I'm sorry'
'Don't be, mum.
'I tried, I simply wasn't good enough.'
He sat up straight and smiled,
Put it all behind him,
And in that instant
Won Gold.

One Minute's Silence

Parents' evening is in full swing.
The buzz of conversation
Echoes through the hall.
We make the rounds of teachers
Sitting at small tables
Discussing progress with attentive
mums and dads.
Quick – the English teacher is free
We dart to her table
Increasingly concerned by the messages
we've heard:
He needs to concentrate more in class,
Organise himself to get his coursework
done.
It's his GCSE year
Whatever are we going to do?

Walking with Angels

The teacher checks her register for latest marks.
Waiting, anticipating more bad news,
My dismayed gaze goes past her shoulder
To a bronze memorial on the wall
Dedicated to ex-pupils who died for their country
In both World Wars.
The list of names is shockingly long.
The teacher looks up, sees the look on my face.
'Yes,' she says quietly,
Without turning round.
'It's awful, isn't it?'
For a full minute
I am silent.

The Torch

I don't want to go yet
Not for a while
I wanted to witness
Your new baby's smile

But we go when we're called
There's no other way
To be with our Lord
At the end of the day

Take over my torch
Brandish it high
Keep the flame burning
Brighten the sky!

Carry my beacon
To the beat of your drum
And entrust it with wisdom
When your time has come.

The Angel

The Angel at the top of the tree
Fluttered its wings
Just once
At me.
A trick of the light –
My logical brain
Sought to explain
And yet, was I right?
It happened again.
Was I tired? Overwrought?
No, but I could not remain
Impassive to this white
Thing my wife had bought.
A wisp of cloth with wings of gauze
Had made me question all the laws
Of reason;
I did not expect
This startling effect
For £1.99
It opened my mind.

The Grandmother – *Still Life with a Teapot*

The Grandmother

If everyone were half as nice
As Mrs Mary (Grandma) Price
The world would be a better place
There'd be more hope for the human race
For she gives out such sound advice
Does Mrs Mary (Grandma) Price.

Young and old and rich and poor
Beat a path to her front door
To hear her wisdom, shed a tear.
With words of solace in their ear
Loads are lightened in a trice
By Mrs Mary (Grandma) Price.

Where to find her? What to do?
Look around, a gran's near you
Invite her for a cup of tea
Tell her your troubles and you'll see
She'll give you just as good advice
As Mrs Mary (Grandma) Price.

Overheard

'Dad hasn't got a tumour!'
Shouted the woman on the train
Down the phone to her mum.
(The signal was bad).
Unable to escape
This positive news
Broadcast to all
I felt kind of sad.
While glad for her dad
How I wished I could say
Those same words
To our sons.
But I couldn't.
I had just found out
That very same day
I would have to change 'hasn't'
To 'has'.

The Scarf

The cheerful red scarf
Stands out
In the crowd
I see it at once
Impossibly
Loud.
But I can't catch him up
He is late
For his job
He quickens his pace
Dodging the mob.
Do I stop, do I run?
I pause to decide –
He might read in my eyes
The bad news I must hide
For a little bit longer –
This evening will do
When we're all together
To see this thing through.
The red scarf bobs on
Zigzagging, weaving,
And I head for home
Having done the right thing.

Twenty Seconds with Wendy Cope

'My name is Claire, please sign it there'
She autographed her book
'I've started writing poems too
Perhaps you'll take a look?
An Irish poet said to me
'You write like Wendy Cope'
And now I meet you face to face
I'm filled with writer's hope.'
She smiled and mustered all her grace
To say, while keeping a straight face
'Send me three, and that's enough
To see if all your talk is puff.'
I really could not ask for more
And fairly skipped out of the door
But then I stopped and pulled up short
Struck by a distressing thought:
Which ones to send? They don't compare
With Wendy's effervescent flair
Perhaps I'll give this chance a miss
I certainly won't send her this.

The French Country House

A pinch of Gallic *je ne sais quoi*
A kilo of confidence, of scale and presence
A *soupçon* of tradition, of history, and stories to tell
A tinge of sadness for times past,
A dollop of laughter, happy families and friends
A lingering aroma of continuity through generations
A long, lazy lunch on a terrace
While lizards flicker in the heat
And warmth exudes from mellow stone.

The Tutu – *Midnight Dancers*

The Tutu

I open the door –
        It's still there.
        A beautiful tutu
        Its bodice surrounded
        With multiple layers of tulle
        In dark blue.
        No one is looking
        What shall I do?
        I pick it up gently
        Hold it against me
        And look in the mirror
        Transfixed by the view.
        For all of ten seconds
        I am a ballerina too!
        I gracefully curtsey…
        Footsteps approach
        I put it back
        Letting go of my dream
        No ballerina
        Has ever been
        Over fifty and size 14.

Soft Outcome

'So,'
Said the Man at the Bank
Shuffling his papers
Embarrassed
'I don't understand.
Why did you invest
In an ISA for him
When you both know
The prognosis?
You can't claim the tax back
The allowance dies too.'
I said very softly
'It improves his morale
Keeps him going.
Small actions like this
Can work wonders
They tell him I believe
It is not over yet
Where on your spreadsheet
Is the column for Hope?
And I left him to his figures.

Yin and Yang

If you were me and I were you
How would we get on as two?
If I were him and she was me,
What would we be like as three?
If we were in a group of four
Or five or six or seven or more
And all put on each others' shoes
Would we win or would we lose?
We may have swapped and changed our name
But we would all come out the same
The total sum of black and white
Of shades of grey, of wrong and right
Would all equate; and there's no doubt
When Vice and Virtue handed out
Uneven helpings on the plate
For some too soon, for some too late
That overall the total sum
Will stay the same till Kingdom Come.

Lovers' Washing

We do it in the kitchen
Taking turns
To put it in
First him, then me.
He pushes all the right buttons
What a turn on
For over half an hour
It lasts, keeps going
Smooth and steady progress
Building a crescendo
Heading inexorably
Towards a noisy climax
Luckily the neighbours are out
And then we are done.
…And so is the washing.

Olympic Opportunity

I never even dreamed it
I never ever planned
To volunteer as a performer
At the best Games in the land.
By chance I found the website
Auditions sounded fun
I clicked and turned up on the date
And danced right through Round One.
The recall was much tougher
'Your rhythm must not drop,
Keep smiling, you can do it
You will come out on top!'
I'd never danced in public
Was the wrong side of fifty
And yet they cast me as a nurse
In the Opening Ceremony.
'The Olympics were for everyone'
I can certainly agree
The Olympics were inclusive
For they included me.

The Cruise

The ship set sail, our hopes were high
For sunny weather, cloudless sky
Ten days of late October sun
Swimming, bathing, having fun.
The Bay of Biscay caused a fright
 A force nine gale howled all night
Replaced by damp cold fog at dawn.
The foghorn, sounding quite forlorn
Wailed for many hours on end
Enough to drive you round the bend.
The passengers became quite dour
The weather made them glum and glower
The corners of their mouths turned down
Three thousand foreheads wore a frown
But on day four the sun came out
They smiled, relaxed, forgot to pout
Bathed in sunshine on the Med
Started tanning, turning red…
Followed by torrential rain
The next two days were just the same
The Captain gave up trying to say
In his announcements at midday

'Tomorrow all will be just fine'
No one would believe that line.
But now they knew just what to do
The Dunkirk spirit shone right through
They'd had a day of sunny weather
So mustn't grumble, stick together
Enjoy ourselves as best we can
Take on the challenge to a man.
Invent more ways of having fun
Instead of scowling, being glum.
The ship returned to its home port
Where sunny skies, by all reports
Had caused a heatwave for ten days
England basked in sunny rays
'Best October we've had yet
But tomorrow will be wet!
Glad I didn't go away
Did you enjoy your holiday?'
Three thousand people got a grip
Presented a stiff upper lip
Were somewhat vague in their replies
While not exactly telling lies
'We had a jolly time together
Didn't always get the weather
Some you win and some you lose
But we had a lovely cruise.'

The Olive Tree

In a Majorcan olive grove
I met an ancient tree
Whose wizened, friendly face
Suggested 'Want advice? Ask me.
I've been around a thousand years
And seen it all before
My wisdom, insight and advice
Is yours – tap on the door.'
I lightly touched the gnarled old trunk
And asked 'Then can you see
The answer to my question:
What is femininity?'
'To be a woman?' 'Yes' I said
'All right, I'll speak at length –
Courage, virtue, vision, bliss
Compassion, wisdom, strength.
This strength can nurture and give birth
Ennoble and empower
Both sexes, who with love and care
Will grow their brightest flower.

A woman teaches as she loves
Inspiring everyone
Her intuition is her guide
She leads, yet makes it fun.'
I smiled and said 'I know that now
You've made it very clear'
And gently touched the light grey bark –
'Like you' she whispered in my ear.

Giving up the Ghost – *Lilies*

Giving up the Ghost

To her very great surprise
Through a veil of tear-filled eyes
She saw her husband's spirit rise
Up from his body to the skies.
Was she dreaming? Suddenly
Her son said, unexpectedly
'His strength has gone right into me'
He could feel what she could see.
She realised that poet knew
When he explains what not to do
'Do not stand by my grave and weep
I am not there, I do not sleep'…
'I am not there.' He saw it too
So when he wrote he also knew
By seeing, feeling, who's to know
He must have sensed the spirit go.
'Give up the Ghost' that age old rhyme
Which has withstood the test of time
Has come to mean 'to give up trying'
When really it's the part of dying
Which matters most; no longer there
The spirit's left and gone Elsewhere.

The Wedding

My husband died
Four days before
The wedding
Of our eldest son
I cried
And then
I took to the floor
And danced
With the bride
While he looked down
On all of us
With loving and paternal pride.

Lunch with a Friend

I was treating her
But she chose from the menu
Just a small plate of squid
Then, suggested I spend
The balance of quid
I'd have paid for the lunch
On some beautiful shoes
In the softest kid
She found in the sale
For me.
So I did.

Christmas Eve

Christmas Eve –
She still hadn't packed
No cards had been written
No presents were wrapped

Then she remembered
With great peace of mind
How friends had been
So wonderfully kind;

They would understand
If just once, for this year,
His family opted
To drop Christmas cheer

And send heartfelt thanks
Through this poem to say
'We'll remember you all
Throughout Christmas Day.'

The Kingfisher

Resplendent in colourful hues
Of orange, azure, emerald, gold
He darts above the surface of the water
Catching fish
Then perches on a bough which dips down to
the river
Cheekily observing two otters at play.
Suddenly, with one swift and graceful flight
He is gone, no more to be seen,
And yet…
Long after he has flown
Long after the river meanders to the sea
An imprint remains
Painted indelibly on the memory:
Flashes of brilliance like water droplets
glistening in the sun
Vivid plumage in bold colours from an artist's
palette
Infusing any scene with charismatic charm
Creating an exuberance which never fades.

Walking with Angels

Today I will walk with angels
I will wander by the sea
Listening to the waves caress the shore
And I will climb the beautiful mountain
Linger in pine scented forest
Breathe the energy of waterfalls.
Above the tree line I will turn and look
Towards the ocean, marvelling
At its silent, tranquil vastness.
Then, gazing at the point where sea meets sky
Blending blues in deepest harmony
I will be uplifted by a thousand wings
Catch glimpses of ethereal mystery
And see him walking with angels
Happy in his new eternity.

Acknowledgements

With grateful thanks to the many people who have encouraged me to compile this book.

Special thanks to my 'cheerleaders':

My husband, Philip
My youngest son, Rob
My mother, Mary
My sister, Karen
Friends Celia, Sylvia, Richard and Adele, Frances, and Lucie and Godfrey
And especially my niece, Katie

Thank you to artist Paola Minekov for permission to reproduce some of her paintings in this book. www.paolaminekov.com

About the *Author*

As a Public Relations consultant and journalist, Claire-Louise Price has dedicated her whole career to promoting the achievements of others. Now it is time to let her own work see the light of day.

Walking with Angels is Claire's first poetry collection.